I0414952

Shut Up
And Write the
Book!

© 2019 Plush Publishing

All rights reserved. No part of this publication may be reproduced, distributed or transmitted in any form or by any means, including photocopying, or other electronic or mechanical methods, without the prior written permission of the publisher, except in the case of brief quotations embodied in critical reviews and certain noncommercial uses permitted by copyright law. ,

Front Cover Image by Adobe Stock

Book Design by Plush Publishing

First Printing Edition 2019

Plush Publishing

P.O. Box 851313

Westland, Michigan 48185

www.plushpublishing.com

~Bring your dream of becoming a best-selling author to life today! ~

As a little girl I always dreamed of writing my very own book. I would sit in my room for hours reading the latest editions of "Nancy Drew" and "The Baby-Sitting Club". As I got older, I became more interested in Urban-Fiction. It wasn't until I went through a domestic violence situation that I decided to pursue my dreams of writing in hopes of my story inspiring other women. Within two months of publishing my first book, I became a best-selling author. How? Actually, it's really not hard as you think. By following a simple writing outline, setting daily writing goals of two-three hours per day and a few secret marketing tips, you can complete and publish a best -selling novel within twelve months (or less if you have more time to set-aside for daily writing goals). This book will give you every piece of information needed to create and publish your book from start to finish in no time at all!

Topics Include:

· **The Four Biggest Mistakes Every New Author Make**

· **Top Secret Marketing Tips to Help Your Book Become a Best Seller. (I Know because I used Them)**

· **A writing outline template that includes plot, character, theme and conflict development, to help structure and build your story.**

· **The Editing Process- What type of editing will your manuscript need?**

· **How to Make Your Synopsis Stand-Out?**

· **Traditional Versus Independent Publishing. Which one will work better for you?**

· **A Monthly Writing Plan used by Best-Selling Authors used to establish deadlines dates to start and a finish each phase of your manuscript.**

*Bonus Writing Journal

Our Goal is to Help Authors Bring Their Vision to Life by polishing their manuscript into the best novel possible before traditionally or self-publishing. Stop Wishing You Were a Best-Selling Author and Become One Today.

The Foundation of
Creating Your Story

The Structure of How to Create A Fictional Story.

There are Four Major components of a Short Story:

- **PLOT-** The action that takes place in the story. It is a series of connected happenings and their result. In order to have a result, we must have an initial event, or conflict.
- **SETTING-** Where, when, and time which the story takes place.
- **CHARACTERS-** Individuals who keep the story going
- **THEME-** The meaning behind the story

Point of View

Point of View is the angle from which the story is told. There are several variations of POV:

First Person - Story told by the main character who interacts closely with the other characters of the book. Speaker uses the pronouns "I", "me", "we". The readers experience the story through the eyes of the main character and only knows how they feel.

Second Person - Story told by a narrator who addresses the reader or some other assumed "you"; speaker uses pronouns "you", "your", and "yours

Third Person - Story told by a narrator who sees all of the action; speaker uses the pronouns "he", "she", "it", "they", "his", "hers", "its", and "theirs". This person may be a character in the story. There are several types of third person POV

Plot Development

Introduction - Beginning of the story; characters, background, and setting revealed.

Rising Action - Events in the story become complicated; the conflict is revealed. These are events between the introduction and climax. •

Conflict - Essential to plot, opposition ties incidents together and moves the plot.

Within a short story, there may be only one central struggle, or there may be many minor obstacles within a dominant struggle.

Internal Conflict
- Struggle within one's self.
- Character vs. Self - Struggles with own soul, physical limitations, choices

External Conflict
- Struggle with a force outside one's self.
- Character vs. Character - Struggles against other people.
- Character vs. Society - Struggles against ideas, practices, or customs of others

Climax

This is the turning point of the story. Readers wonders what will happen next; will the conflict be resolved or not?

- Main character receives new information.
- Main character accepts this information (realizes it but does not necessarily agree with it).
- Main character acts on this information
- Falling action - Resolution begins; events and complications start to fall into place. These are the events between climax and denouement.
- Resolution (Conclusion) - Final outcome of events in the story.

Plot Techniques

Suspense - feeling of excitement or tension the reader experiences as the plot unfolds. Writers create suspense by raising questions in the reader's mind.

Foreshadowing - a hint or clue about an event that will occur later in the story.

Flashback - a section of the story that is interrupted to tell about an earlier event.

Surprise Ending - an ending that catches the reader off guard with something unexpected.

Setting

Location that a story takes place. For some stories, the setting is very important; while for others, it is not. When examining how setting contributes to a story, there are multiple aspects to consider:

Place - Geographical location; where is the action of the story taking place?

Time - Historical period, time of day, year, when is the story taking place? 3

Social conditions - What is the daily life of the character's like?

Mood or atmosphere - What feeling is created at the beginning of the story? Cheerful or eerie?

Character Development

Types of Fictional Characters

Major characters- are vital to the development and resolution of the conflict.

Minor characters- reinforce major characters to help move the plot events forward.

There are four types of characters in fiction

Round - Fully developed personalities that are affected by the story's events; they can learn, grow, or deteriorate by the end of the story. Characters are most convincing when they resemble real people by being consistent, motivated, and life-like.

Flat - One-dimensional character

Dynamic - Character who does go through change and "grows" during a story

Static - Character does not go through a change.

Protagonist and Antagonist Characters

Now that you have established your characters, the next step is deciding your protagonist and antagonist of the story. Protagonists and antagonists are key to engaging readers by creating tension throughout the story.

Protagonist

- Clear center of story; all major events are important to this character.
- Attempts to accomplish something
- Usually is as a good person and the hero of the story

Antagonist

- Opposition or "enemy" of main character.
- Character who wants something in opposition to the protagonist
- Normally the bad person or villain of the story. But remember they are not completely "bad". They are more complicated and flawed which will makes them relatable to the reader.

Theme

Themes are the central focus of the story. A story theme is what helps to express the intended lesson, conclusion, message, or point of view of the author. Themes connect all the parts of the story such as characters, plot, conflict, setting, and event.

Common Fictional Novel Themes Are:

- Love
- Death.
- Good vs. evil.
- Power and corruption
- Survival
- Courage and heroism.

Characteristic Examples

active

adventurous

affectionate

alert

ambitious

angry

annoyed

anxious

arrogant

attentive

careful

careless

cautious

charming

cheerful

demanding

dependable

depressed

determined

discouraged

dishonest

disrespectful

doubtful

dull

eager

easygoing

energetic

evil

Good

Happy

Honest

Impatient

Independent

Innocent

Kind

Lazy

Lonely

Loving

Loyal

Mature

Mean

Messy

Nice

Obnoxious

Peaceful

Pleasant

Polite

Poor

Positive

Rational

Reliable

Religious

Rich

Rough

Secretive

Selfish

Shy

Silly

Smart

Sneaky

Spoiled

Stingy

Strange

Stubborn

Sweet

Thoughtful

Trustworthy

Unhappy

Upset

Weak

Wise

Wrong

Let's Start Writing!

Goal Outline

Start Date:

Desired End Date:

Manuscript Word Count:

Possible Chapter Count:

Target Audience:

Story Foundation

Title

When and Where Does the Story Take Place?

Basic Summary

Describe the Basic Idea of Your Story in 1-2 Paragraphs

Desired Number of Chapters

Plot Development

Give a Brief Description of the Plot.

How Does the Story Begin?

How Does the Story End?

How Events Unfold and Escalate?

How Does the Story End?

Where Will the Story Take Place?

During What Time?

What Problems Will the Characters Face?

Character Development

Who Is Your Main Character?

Are they a Protagonist or Antagonist Character?

Who Is Your Supporting Character?

Are they a Protagonist or Antagonist Character?

Building Your Character

Main Character

Character Full Name:

Character Nickname:

Character Appearance:

Age:

How old does s/he appear?

Eye Color:

Glasses or contacts:

Weight:

Height:

Type of body/build:

Skin tone:

Skin type:

Shape of face:

Distinguishing Marks:

Predominant feature:

Looks like:

Building Your Character

Secondary Character

Character Full Name:

Character Nickname:

Character Appearance:

Age:

How old does s/he appear?

Eye Color:

Glasses or contacts:

Weight:

Height:

Type of body/build:

Skin tone:

Skin type:

Shape of face:

Distinguishing Marks:

Predominant feature:

Looks like:

Character Qualities

Greatest source of strength.

Greatest source of weakness.

What Flaws Do They Have?

What do they need to overcome?

What Past Events Shaped Them into Who They Are?

Character's soft spot?

Is this soft spot obvious to others?

If not, how does character hide it?

Biggest vulnerability?

How does character react in a crisis?

How does character face problems?

Kinds of problems character usually runs into:

How does character react to new problems?

How does character react to change?

Why does s/he have this problem/crisis?

How will s/he react to this problem?

Will facing the problem change him/her in any way?

Character flaws:

Mannerisms:

Biggest regret:

Minor regrets:

Biggest accomplishment:

Minor accomplishments:

Character's darkest secret:

Does anyone else know?

Character Creations

Favorite clothing & Why?

Least favorite clothing & Why?

Jewelry & Other accessories?

Where does character live?

Plot Development

Step 1

What is the main problem your character must solve?

What Important Goal do your character have to solve?

Why is this problem or goal important to your main character?

Step 2

What Barriers do your main character face in solving their
problem?

How has the main character changed from the beginning
of the story

Step 3

What are the main events that will move your main character closer or further away from accomplishing their goal?

At least two secondary characters should be incorporated into this.

Step 4

Why does the story end?

How does the story end?

What is in the characters future?

What is the ending for the Protagonist   character?

What is the ending for the antagonist character?

Do you want an unexpected ending?

If so what?

What is the final feeling you want the readers to walk away with?

What message do you want the readers to walk away with?

Rising Action

Events in the story become complicated

Place a Character in Trouble

Give New Meaning to a Past Scene

Deepen A meaning to Something

Bring more attention to a Minor Character

Conflict

Essential to plot, opposition ties incidents together and moves the plot.

Resolution

The Climax or Ending where the problem is resolved which includes a description of the final ending.

Develop the Root of Your Story

Introduction

Scene 1

What Characters are involved?

Where does the scene take place?

What happens next?

Scene 2

What Characters are involved?

Where does the scene take place?

What happens next?

Scene 3

What Characters are involved?

Where does the scene take place?

What happens next?

Scene 4

What Characters are involved?

Where does the scene take place?

What happens next?

Complications

A dilemma or problem that sets of a sequence of interesting events

Scene 1

Scene 2

Scene 3

Scene 4

Sequence of Events

Triggered by the Complications

Scene 1

First...

Next ...

Later...

After...

Scene 2

First...

Next ...

Later...

After...

Scene 3

First...

Next ...

Later...

After...

Scene 4

First...

Next ...

Later...

After...

Potential Plot Twist

Some Identity Is Mistaken

Someone Has a Secret Agenda

Critical Information Is Missing

How does this twist surprise the reader or character?

How does this information change the outcome of the story?

How to Develop a Fight Scene

Who Gets Involved in the Fight?

Why do they start fighting?

Do all parties fight fair?

Where do they fight?

How does the fight play out?

Do they have weapons?

Is anyone injured or killed?

Are there any onlookers or instigators?

Why is at stake for each person?

Could the problem had been resolved without fighting?

How does the fight end?

What happens after the fight Does the fight end the conflict between them?

Synopsis Development

Now Here Comes the Hard Part! Writing Your Synopsis! Your Synopsis Is More Important Than the Book Content Itself. It Should Scream,

"Read Me!"

There are more then a million books published in the United States alone. Your synopsis is what will get your book in the hands of the readers. Consider your synopsis as your book sales pitch. A well-written synopsis is critical to draw in readers and convince them to buy your book.

What is a Synopsis?

A synopsis is a teaser of your manuscript. It should be engaging, mysterious and catchy enough to stand out and grab the readers attention and reel them in.

Your synopsis should be short (75-150 Words)

Do's

Keep it short

Hint at a cliffhanger

Make it Relatable to the reader

Do Not's

Include a list of every character in the book

Be misleading

Give the ending away

How to Create A Synopsis

List the Main Plot Points?

What are the Main Revelations?

How can you tease or mislead the readers?

What sort of readers do you want for your story?

What Words Will Appeal to the reader?

Do you need to warn the reader about anything?

Writing Coach

A writing coach is someone who encourages you and holds you accountable to finishing your book. They might set deadlines for you, conference calls with you, and will probably give you a writing plan or schedule to follow. Most writing coaches will also provide feedback on your work as you finish it, usually with a focus on big picture elements. Your Writing Coach Will Also Help You Set Deadlines dates to start and a finish each phase of your manuscript. Each phase of your writing project should have a day you begin that phase and a day you complete it.

The Editing Process

~The type of editing an author requires for their manuscript will depend on their writing level. ~

Manuscript Assessment

(The Writing Stage)

Manuscript Assessment is a Detailed Feedback on a Manuscript. This feedback lets the author know the positives/strengths and negatives/weakness of the manuscript. The editor will provide insight as to whether readers will perceive the story as the author intended and give advice on how to improve the story. This service does not include problem solving or frequent content issues. Advice will be specific to the types of issues present in the manuscript, but the advice will often be somewhat generic and point to references where the author can further study-up on a skill or concept on their own.

Developmental Editing

(The Rough Draft Stage)

Developmental Editing assists the author with the organization, layout, and delivery of their message. A developmental editor may revise the document as a whole. It involves tightening and clarifying sentences, paragraphs, chapters and scenes. Are the chapters and paragraphs in the right order? Are there any places in the book that are unexplainable? Are there holes in the information or story presented? Are the characters likable? During this editing process full sentences and paragraphs can be added, removed, shortened or elaborated on. Developmental Editing helps to bring the story characters and plots to life.

Line editing

(Revision Stage)

The process of assessing the manuscript "as a whole", considering its tone, accuracy, clarity, consistency and overall effectiveness. Line editing helps ensure a work's argument and main points are clear and well-supported. Line editors expand their efforts to suggest changes to make sentences crisper and tighter by fixing redundancy and verbosity issues, while improving awkward sentence and paragraph construction without a full rewrite. Your editor is going to identify and fix any problems or suggest ways you can revise a word, sentence, or paragraph.

Copy Editing

(Review Stage)

This is a light form of editing that applies a professional polish to a book. The editor reviews your work, fixing any mechanical errors in spelling, grammar, and punctuation. Copy editing also checks for inconsistency within the story. This includes character description, plot points, and setting. Does each character stay true to his own description throughout the story? Are there conflicting descriptions of the house? For example, have you described the setting as "Michelle blue eyes" on one page but "Michelle chestnut hazel eyes" on another page? (Yes, it happens quite often)

Proof Reading

(The Final Revision Stage)

Works with the Final draft already formatted, just prior to publication. Proofreading is intended to pick up the final typos and spelling mistakes and to correct inconsistencies, like making sure the word "proofreading" is always spelled as one word and not "proof-reading" or "proof reading. Manuscripts should have at least one form of Editing (Copy or Line) completed before the Proofreading process. During the proofreading stage minor errors are corrected such as spelling, grammar, punctuation and typos. This is the final step of the editorial process before print and no manuscript details changes are made. *A proofreader isn't looking to fix your content—just correcting any grammatical errors they see.

To Summarize the Editing Process:

*Copyeditors catch all the mistakes the author missed. Proofreaders catch all the mistakes the copyeditor missed.

*Once the copyediting is done, then you go to proofreading

*A proofreader isn't looking to fix your content—just correcting any grammatical errors they see.

Formatting

The editor will amend document text to ensure that it complies with the required format.

How Should I Publish My Book?

Your Manuscript is Finished, Polished and Ready to Be Published. Now its time to decide which type of Publishing will work best for you.

Traditional Versus Independent Publishing

To publish with a major publishing house, you will normally be required to submit the first three chapters of your manuscript along with your synopsis for review. An editor within the publishing company will read it over and decide whether to offer the author a deal. Traditional publishing book deals usually involve the publishing company purchasing the book's rights from the author. In exchange, the author will receive royalties. Royalties are normally based off authors previous experience. Royalty rates are a percentage of the sale of the book. Typically, new authors are not offered advanced royalties and earn an average of sixty percent royalties.

Traditional Publishing

Pros

- There is no upfront cost. Editors, cover designers, formatters and marketing cost are typically provided by the publishing company.
- Professional Marketing, Advertisement and Distribution of Book

Cons

- Publication is a slow process. Due to an extensive editing process
- Loss of creative control.

Independent Publishing

Pros

- Fast publication process. Once completed your book can be on sale on Amazon within four hours and then you can be paid 60 days later.
- Author receive one hundred percent of their royalties.

Cons

- You will be responsible for the upfront cost of editing, designing, marketing, and distributing your book.
- Lack of significant marketing help.

The determining factor in deciding if you should traditionally or Independently will depend on two main factors:

A) How much editing you book will need?

The editing process is typically the most expensive part of self-publishing. If you have strong creativity and writing skills, your manuscript may not require much editing which means independently publishing could be your best option.

B) Do you have a strong enough platform to market, advertise, and distribute your book on your own? If so, independently publishing could be your best option.

The Four Biggest Mistakes to Avoid in Self-Publishing

As a new author mistakes are bound to happen! But some common mistakes can kill your career before it even starts.

1) Bad Book Cover

The saying is true! People judge a book by its cover. If your book cover isn't persuasive and exciting, then people won't buy it. Simple!

2) Over Pricing Your First Book

The average price of eBooks for *new authors* range from $0.99 to $2.99. For paperbacks the average cost is $3.99-$5.99. As the interest of your book increase you can increase the price as well. I know you are thinking "My Book Is Worth More!", and you are probable correct. But as with any new job or venture you must start from the bottom and work your way up.

3) Lack of Proper Manuscript Editing

With over 500,000 books published per year, proper editing of your manuscript will help to create a book the reader can't put down which is crucial for the success of self-published books. It is impossible for readers to concentrate on your story if it is filled with grammatical errors.

Actual Kindle Review
September 28, 2017
Format: Kindle Edition Verified Purchase
"This book might have stood a better chance if it were proofread. There are grammatical mistakes and it jumped around that I often had to read paragraphs more than once."

4) Underestimating the power of Reviews

Reviews directly influence how your self-published book will rank and sell on Amazon. Readers are more likely to buy books with good reviews. Having at least fifteen friends and family ready to review your book during the first few days of its launch can greatly increase overall book sales.

Self-publishing a book is a great achievement. The process is exciting and thrilling but can be a challenge as well. Always keep in mind; Success comes with a few failures!

Secret Marketing Tips

If you decide to self-publish, you will be responsible for the tasks a traditional publisher would typically take on including marketing and advertising your book. That means you not only have to write a great book, but you also take on the job of marketing and promoting it. However, most self-published authors do not have large marketing budgets to pay for excessive book marketing campaigns. The great news is you don't have to spend massive amounts of money to have your book reach hundreds of readers per day. With little as $1 a day, you can tremendously increase your book sales and strengthen your author platform through social media advertisement. Facebook is the preferred place for 97% of marketers to run paid ads because it provides the ability to target specific people who are most likely to buy your product. Simply select your audience based on their interest.

How to Create Your Marketing Target Audience

The categories I have found with the most engaging audience and who have the highest potential to purchase self-published books are:

- Readers
- Kindle Readers
- Kindle Fire
- eBooks
- Amazon Kindle
- Literature and
- Short Story

*I increased by book sales by 90% and became a Best-Seller Author within two months by simply creating a $1 per day marketing campaign on Facebook.

Join Book Groups on Social Media

Did you know there are over one thousand Book Groups on Social Media where you can advertise your book for FREE to readers across the world.

For Facebook simply go to your search bar and type in "Book Groups". From there send a request to join. Most Book Clubs approvals are fast and easy. For a few, you will be asked two to three basic questions regarding why you are requesting to join the group. Be honest! Simply state you are a new author looking to expand your platform. Once you are approved, you will be able to promote your book for free at least **once per day.** This is an excellent way for new authors to meet new readers! Depending on the genre you are writing in, you can narrow your search down to find your specific target audience. For example, if you are an urban fiction author, type "Urban Book Clubs" into your search bar. I have found the following Book Groups on Facebook to have the most engaging readers who are always looking for new books to read.

- I Love Urban Fiction Book Club
- Book Club: Urban Fiction
- Die Hard Readers Group
- Book Alliance
- Book Lovers
- Book Promo
- Book Love and Promotions
- Readers Club
- Book Beast Promotions
- Book Lovers
- Ready to Read

It is also important to add at least one new author *"per day"* to your social media account! This is a great way to network with a variety of authors. You are probably asking yourself; How do I find other authors? Again, the simplest way to find other authors on social media is by using your search bar. Type "Authors", into your search bar and a list of authors will appear. Feel free to start with me:

Facebook @ Ms. L.B.

Instagram @ author_ms_lb

You will notice, as you add more authors, more authors will appear under "people you may know" (Facebook) or "suggested people to follow" (Instagram). It is important to network with as many authors as possible.

Add Book Links

"You Lose a Reader when They Lose Patience!" This is a small detail that a lot of new authors miss. Your book must be quick and easy for the reader to find! The best way to accomplish this is by attaching your *"One Click Link"* to all promotional or marketing advertisement. Your One click link is also known as an ASIN.

Example: For My Novel "He Played Me"

ASIN: B07QLJNH6M

If you are self-publishing your ASIN will only be made available to you once your book goes live *or* if you decide to set your book up for pre-order purchases.

If you are traditionally publishing request your ASIN from your publisher as soon as possible.

Have a Promotional Video Trailer Created for Your Book!

Video trailers are rapidly becoming the newest way to promote your book and grab new readers. If a Picture say a thousand words, a video trailer says a million. The average cost to create a video trailer can range between $50.00 -$100.00. However, research has shown promotional video trailers have the potential to increase book sales by over eighty percent.

Hashtags

Making yourself stand out among 800 million Social Media users is not an easy task. Hashtags play a crucial role in developing an interest of your social media platform. They make it easier for people to identify and find you/your brand. The more you use hashtags the greater your chances are of growing your audience.

Examples of good book hashtags to use are:

#Booklovers

#Book Addicts

#Bookworms

#Always Reading

#Goodreads

Setting Daily Writing Goals

Create a Writer's Notebook

Write in this notebook 10 minutes each day. Jot down ideas that could possibly make a good story. When an idea comes to you from reading a newspaper story, watching television, or walking through a mall – write it down. You don't need to write in complete sentences. It only needs to make sense to you, something to jog your memory.

Month 1

Title

When and Where Does the Story Take Place?

Basic Summary

Describe the Basic Idea of Your Story in 1-2 Paragraphs

Month 2

Plot Development

Give a Brief Description of the Plot

How Does the Story Begin?

How Does the Story End?

<u>Month 3</u>

How the Events Unfold and Escalate

How Does the Story End?

Where Will the Story Take Place?

During What Time?

What Problems Will the Character Faces?

Month 4

Character Building

Who Is Your Main Character?

Are they a Protagonist or Antagonist Character?

Who Is Your Supporting Character?

Are they a Protagonist or Antagonist Character?

Build Main Character Profile

Build Secondary Character profile

What is the main problem your character must solve?

What Important Goal do your character have to solve?

Why is this problem or goal important to your main
character?

Month 5

Plot Development

What Barriers do your main character face in solving their problem?

How has the main character changed from the beginning of the story

What are the main events that will move your main character closer or further away from accomplishing their goal?

At least two secondary characters should be incorporated into this.

Month 6

Why does the story end?

How does the story end?

What is in the characters future?

What is the ending for the Protagonist   character?

What is the ending for the antagonist character?

Do you want an unexpected ending?

If so what?

What is the final feeling you want the readers to walk away with?

What message do you want the readers to walk away with?

Month 7

Rising Action

Events in the story become complicated

Place a Character in Trouble

Give New Meaning to a Past Scene

Deepen A meaning to Something

Bring more attention to a Minor Character

Month 8

Conflict

Essential to plot, opposition ties incidents together and moves the plot.

Month 9

Conflict Resolution

The Climax or Ending where the problem is resolved which includes a description of the final ending.

Month 10

1) Synopsis Development

- List the Main Plot Points?
- What are the Main Revelations?
- How can you tease or mislead the readers?
- What sort of readers do you want for your story?
- What Words Will Appeal to the reader?
- Do you need to warn the reader about anything?

2) Rough Draft Creation

3) *Editing Stage of Manuscript*

Manuscript Assessment

Developmental Editing

Month 11

Revision of Manuscript

Editing Stage of Manuscript

~Line editing~

The process of assessing the manuscript "as a whole", considering its tone, accuracy, clarity, consistency and overall effectiveness. Line editing helps ensure a work's argument and main points are clear and well-supported.

Review of Manuscript

Editing Stage of Manuscript

~Copy Editing~

This is a light form of editing that applies a professional polish to a book. The editor reviews your work, fixing any mechanical errors in spelling, grammar, and punctuation.

Month 12

Manuscript Final Revision

Editing Stage of Manuscript

~Proofreading~

Manuscripts should have at least one form of Editing (Copy or Line) completed before being Proofreading process. During the proofreading stage minor errors are corrected such as spelling, grammar, punctuation and typos. This is the final step of the editorial process before print and no manuscript details changes are made.

Writing Journal

www.ingramcontent.com/pod-product-compliance
Lightning Source LLC
Chambersburg PA
CBHW031235280526
45784CB00004B/1584